UNTIL HE COMES AGAIN

FATHER JACK SPAULDING

UNTIL HE COMES AGAIN

FATHER JACK SPAULDING

Queenship

PUBLISHING COMPANY
P.O. Box 220 • Goleta, CA 93116
(800) 647-9882 • (805) 692-0043 • Fax: (805) 967-5133

A special thanks to Mrs. Trary Barnes of Immaculata
Parish in St. Louis, Missouri for taping the talks that
made this book possible.

Library of Congress Number # 2002095720

Published by:
    Queenship Publishing
    P.O. Box 220
    Goleta, CA 93116
    (800) 647-9882 • (805) 692-0043 • Fax: (805) 967-5133

Printed in the United States of America

ISBN: 1-57918-222-4

Cover photo - Deacon Len Zbiegien

TABLE OF CONTENTS

"What we await are new heavens and a new earth where, according to
His promise, the justice of God will reside. So, beloved, while waiting
For this, make every effort to be found without stain or defilement,
And at peace in His sight. Consider that Our Lord's patience is directed
Toward salvation."

2 Peter 3: 13-15a

INTRODUCTION

This book, *UNTIL HE COMES AGAIN,* is a sequel to my first, *HOPE FOR THE JOURNEY.* Both books are basically the written version of some of the conferences I've presented for days of recollection and parish retreats throughout the country. This book includes talks given since the first book was published in 1995.

The purpose of this book is really the same as that of the first: to bring hope, understanding, peace and enthusiasm to all of us as we try to follow Our Lord Jesus Christ. However, this book, I think, may bring something in addition. Before this new millennium began there was a lot of speculation and even trepidation as to what would happen to the world when the calendar turned 2000 A.D. (for the purists, 2001 A.D.). Many thought for certain the new millennium would usher in the Second Coming of Jesus and so these were preparing in earnest to meet their Savior. Most people simply waited to see what, if anything, would happen. As we who lived through this "passage" can attest, everyone breathed a little easier when those days came and went; and things got back to "normal." Then came September, 11, 2001. With the destruction of the Twin World Trade Towers in New York City, the attack on the Pentagon, and the third terrorist attack aborted in a field in Pennsylvania, we Americans and the entire world seemed to have been frozen in time, in disbelief, that anything that horrific could happen, especially here in the United States of America. Again, as we who lived through this "passage" can attest, from that day on "normal" will never be the same. The world and the way especially we Americans look at the world has changed. The jury is still out on whether this change will be for the good or not.

These events are the background and the reason for this book. I hope to shed some light on and offer some suggestions as to how we live from now on. Jesus didn't return in the way many had thought or had hoped He would at the beginning of the Third Millennium. So, what do we do, how does Jesus want us to live until He comes again? In the pages of this little book we will see that He wants us to: say yes to God; keep the main thing the main thing; not be "nice," be Catholic; carry the cross of holiness; look again at the Ten Commandments; and, most importantly, to realize that God only knows.

We can be reassured through the gift of our Faith that we are never alone. Even in the most horrible and frightening events in our personal lives or in the life or our country and of our world, Jesus reminds us: "Do not be afraid.... I am with you always until the end of the world." For this reason we will be joyful in the midst of sorrow, courageous in the midst of fear, hopeful in times of despair, and filled with peace when the wicked rage and roar, **UNTIL HE COMES AGAIN!**

Fr. Jack Spaulding
Phoenix, Arizona
July 27, 2002

Y to G (Yes to God)

PSALM 139

O Lord, you have probed me and you know me; you know when I sit and when I stand; you understand my thoughts from afar.

My journeys and my quest you scrutinize, with all my ways you are familiar.

Even before a word is on my tongue, behold, O lord, you know the whole of it.

Behind me and before, you hem me in and rest your hand upon me.

Such knowledge is too wonderful for me; too lofty for me to attain.

Where can I go from your spirit? From your presence where can I flee?

If I go up to the heavens, you are there; if I sink to the netherworld, you are present there.

If I take the wings of the dawn, if I settle at the farthest limits of the sea, even there your hand shall guide me.

If I say, "Surely the darkness shall hide me, and night shall be my light—"

For you darkness itself is not dark, and night shines as the day.

(Darkness and light are the same.)

Truly you have formed my inmost being; you knit me in my mother's womb.

I give you thanks that I am fearfully, wonderfully made; wonderful are your works.

My soul also you knew full well; nor was my frame unknown to you when I was made in secret, when I was fashioned in the depths of the earth.

Your eyes have seen my actions; in your book they are well written; my days were limited before one of them existed.

How weighty are your designs, O God; how vast the sum of them!

Were I to recount them, they would outnumber the sands; did I reach the end of them, I should still be with you.

If only you would destroy the wicked, O God, and the men of blood were to depart from me!

Wickedly they invoke your name; your foes swear faithless oaths.

Do I not hate, O Lord, those who hate you? Those who rise up against you do I not loathe?

With a deadly hatred I hate them; they are my enemies.

Probe me, O God, and know my heart; try me, and know my thoughts;

See if my way is crooked, and lead me in the way of old.

As we look at our relationship with God in this new millennium, I want to look at some of the things we have known all of our lives that perhaps we haven't reflected upon recently. I'm sure that most of you have at least heard of the book that was written a few years ago by the title: *All I Ever Needed to Know I Learned In Kindergarten.* There is certainly a lot of truth in this little book; and, I believe, applying this same reasoning to our faith, what we need to know about Our Lord, Jesus, has already been placed deep within our heart by God, Our Father. We simply need to reflect quietly more often and listen to God speak to our heart. This in itself can be a real challenge today, especially as we plummet headlong into the new millennium. As you know there were all kinds of hype having to do with the calendar turning to the year 2000. The Y2K phenomenon had many people literally and figuratively running for the hills. We were encouraged to save food and water, and wait for all of the computers to shut down. For many, waiting for the year 2000 was a frightening experience.

There were numerous suggestions for preparing for this new millennium. One of the best, I think, was given by our eighth grade class of the year 2000. Each year the graduating class gives a theme to their graduating year for the whole school. The theme given to the year 2000 was "Y to G," which stood for "yes to God." When the eighth graders told me what they had chosen for the theme of their school year, I thought, "That's it! That's the way to prepare for the new millennium! Say "yes" to God!" Actually, this is the only way to really live our lives in this or in any other millennium. So, with this little phrase in mind, let's take a good look at how we do say "yes" to God.

Saying, "yes" to God is not as simple as it sounds; or, I should say, it's not as easy as it sounds. It isn't easy saying "yes" to Him because that usually means saying "no" to something or to someone—the "someone" is most often ourselves. When we say yes to God what we're really saying is, "You're God, and I am not." I would suggest that you read Psalm 139 now before you continue reading any more of this chapter. This beautiful psalm sets the tone and the rationale for saying yes to God. The great gift of this psalm is very simply remembering that God is the One Who is really in control of everything. To put this in the worldly vernacular, God's been around for a long time—in fact, He always was, always is, and always will be. He has no intention of retiring. He's very good at what He does, and, if we would just allow Him to do what He does best, i.e. be God; we'd all be better off. In saying yes to God we allow Him to be Who He is. Now, that may seem like a very strange statement because we know that God's going to be God whether we "allow" Him to be God or not. The fact is, however, when we don't choose to allow God to be God in our lives, then *we* become the god of our lives, and that doesn't work so well. When I become the god of my life, I try to control whatever is happening to me. This, in itself, would be bad enough, but what usually happens is that, when I become the god of my life, then I try to be the god of other peoples' lives too, especially the lives of my family members. How about you? When we begin to take control then God simply steps back and waits because there really can only be one God in our lives. Many times when people say, "I just don't feel God's presence anymore," my response is to quote a bumper sticker I saw which says: "If you feel far from God, guess who moved?" The more we take control of our lives or the lives of our family or friends, the more God steps back. Conversely, the more we say to Him, "Lord, I want you in my life. I need you in my life. I need and want you to walk with me every step of the way this side of heaven," He is with us whether we *feel* His presence or not. If we allow God to be the God of our lives, then everything does work out. Maybe not the way we had planned them to work or the way we would like them to work; but when God is the God of our lives then everything works to the good, as the old saying goes: "God writes straight with our crooked lines."

In that beautiful Psalm 139 we see a very wonderful statement, really a declaration to the effect that maybe we have limited God. God is so loving that He will never force Himself on us. At times, if we are honest with ourselves, we see by our attitude that we are creating God into an image with which we can feel comfortable. However, the reality is that God is *not* to be our comfort zone or our security blanket. He is not the Someone to blame when everything goes wrong, i.e. not the way we had planned and manipulated them to go. The *reality* is that He created us; we did not created Him! He is not a figment of our imagination or the "opiate of the masses." We have been created into His image and likeness, not the other way around. God is a crazy-in-love-with-us God. He is beyond our comprehension! Consider, if you will, what Jesus says to us about God, the Father. In the parables when He talks about the Father, Jesus shows us things about Him that are simply not logical. When He tells us of the shepherd who has 100 sheep and loses one of them, Jesus says that the Good Shepherd leaves the 99 to search and find the lost one. Something like that is absolutely crazy by today's standards. What would we do? We'd probably write the one off as a tax loss. But not God the Father. That's the kind of God He is. In that same section of the Gospel the next parable talks about the woman who has ten coins and loses one of them. She searches the whole house until she finds the lost coin and then invites her neighbors in to celebrate with her. We'd never do that. We'd probably blame someone else for the loss and go on with our lives. After all it was only one coin; we have nine left. God doesn't do it that way. He writes off no one because He has written each of us in the palm of His hand! We are so dear to Him that He has numbered the hairs on our head, the days of our lives, and each breath we take. That's how much He loves us! What hits me so hard sometimes is that my very trying to understand Him limits what He wants to do for me. Because we can't understand what He is doing or how He is doing it, we believe it just can't happen. Our Blessed Mother, as always, is one of our best role models in saying yes to God. When the archangel Gabriel appeared to her, telling her of what God had planned for her life, Mary humbly stated that she didn't know how anything like that could happen, given her life situation. When the angel explained to her how everything was going to take place, she still didn't understand but she said yes because she trusted that God knew what He was doing. Remember? "Behold the handmaid of the Lord. Be it done to me according to Your word." She said yes, yes to God. That "yes" made all the difference in the world and for the world, literally! Basically, Our Blessed Mother said very simply, "Lord, I don't understand you, but I trust you!" Wouldn't it be great if we could come to a point in our lives where that could be our constant response to God, instead of trying to control the whole world and then going berserk when things don't go the way we want them to!

I believe that the greatest challenge most of us face in allowing God to be God and not taking the control back from Him is with our families. Those of you who are parents know how difficult it can be not to try to live your childrens' lives for them. It is truly a holy balancing act, especially when you have teenagers, to guide them without smothering them as you instill in them firm moral character and an appreciation of the Faith. The temptation is constant to give in when "everybody is doing" whatever your teen is saying that everybody is doing. If you have to choose between being your children's friend and being their parent, there is *no* choice. It is interesting, however, when we listen to ourselves say to them, "If you would just do what I tell you, you wouldn't get into so much trouble. Listen to me. I know what I'm saying."Isn't that what God says to us all the time? If we expect obedience from our children, and we should, do they see us being obedient to God? If we expect them to say yes to us, and we should, do they see us saying yes to God in what we say and do? When we, as adults, begin saying yes to God by the way we live, that will have a rippling affect in our families. We will be preaching the truth of the Gospel, as St. Francis of Assisi said, "and sometimes we will use words."

Beginning to live our lives saying yes to God will not come easy at first; but, as with any habit, the more we practice the better we become. The wonderful thing that we, as Catholic Christians, have is the example of the saints. These men and women went through the same battles with control as we are going through. They know the struggles and the temptation to take over God's role in our lives. We need to ask for their prayers and we need to follow their example. How they did it. You can certainly choose any saint you wish; I would suggest two for starters. One is already canonized (officially recognized as a saint with "St." in front of her name), St. Therese of Lisieux. The other is not canonized yet, Mother Teresa of Calcutta. The first died when she was 24;

the second died just a few years ago at the age of 82. St. Therese was a cloistered Carmelite nun, who never left the Carmel. Mother Teresa, who chose that name because she wanted St. Therese to be her special patroness, founded the Missionaries of Charity at age 38 after being a Presentation Sister for a number of years, and began working in Calcutta, India, with the poorest of the poor. Her work and her sisters have since spread worldwide, and she won the Nobel Peace Prize. What these two holy women shared with every ounce of their being was an all-consuming love for Jesus Christ and the willingness to say yes to whatever He asked of them. If you haven't read St. Therese's autobiography, *The Story of a Soul,* I recommend you do. This book, which she wrote in obedience to her superior's request, is full of one story after another of how she said yes each day in little ways to surrender her heart to her Love, Jesus. She realized early on that she was not cut out to perform heroic acts like many of the saints whose lives she read. What came to her after reading St. Paul's letter to the Corinthians, chapter 13, was that she was called to love with all of her heart all the time and in every circumstance in her life as a Carmelite nun. When you read her story you will see that you can do what she did. It is the simple thing, the little self-sacrifice, the little saying no to yourself, the little act of kindness that each one of us is more than capable of doing with the Lord's help. This is what it means to say yes to God.

Mother Teresa's life in many ways was very different from that of her patroness; but in the things that really mattered, they were exactly the same. One of the things that Mother Teresa said constantly was: "Do little things with great love." These "little things" will be noticed by no one but God. This was exactly what her life was composed of, little acts filled with great love. One time she was asked how she could constantly take care of the sick and the dying, the poorest of the poor. Her response was simple and direct: "I am only and always taking care of Jesus, who comes to me in the distressing disguise of the poorest of the poor." None of us is called to take care of the poorest of the poor in Calcutta. No, again as Mother Teresa reminded us, our "Calcutta" is our own home, our own neighborhood, our own parish; and our "poorest of the poor" is our own family, our relatives, friends, and parishioners, anyone who needs us. We can do these "little things with great love." As we will discover, this will simply mean saying no to ourselves and yes to God as He comes to us in the sometimes inconvenient and irritating disguise of our spouse, child, relative, friend, or stranger. If you need biblical backup for how Our Lord looks at this way of acting, I refer you to St. Matthew's Gospel and his beautiful account of the last judgment: "When did we see You hungry or thirsty or naked or ill or in prison or away from home? Then the King shall say, "As often as you did it/didn't do it for the least of my brothers or sisters you did it/didn't do it for Me!'" Mother Teresa grasped very well what Jesus was and is still saying in this section of Matthew's Gospel. It will be the little things done with great love, which will take us from here to eternity!

It occurs to me that if we wait for the time in our lives when Jesus asks for a big yes from us we will miss all of the little "yeses" that He is asking of us everyday. It is this "ordinary holiness," the everyday saying yes to Jesus and no to ourselves (if that's what it takes to say yes to Him), which will bring us to heaven. It will also give us a tremendous freedom here on earth. It will bring us peace and joy and the serenity, which only comes when we surrender to God. This is the gift which God, Our Father, and Jesus, Our Savior, have waiting for us. It is ours for the taking!

The various ways of saying yes to God, which we have discussed up to this point, have been practical and, I hope, based in solid spirituality. What I am now going to propose for your consideration is an area, which, perhaps, most people don't even consider when they think about turning their lives over to God. To be very honest I, myself, didn't. In fact, for years I refused to turn this part of my life over to Him. What is this area not given to God? Our **money!** Up until about eight years ago I had the attitude: "Lord, I'm your priest. I've given you my entire life. You want my money too?" The answer came loudly and clearly, **"YES!"** I'm convinced, from personal experience, that we cannot really say a complete yes to God, we cannot fully turn our entire lives over to God, until we are obedient to Him in how He asks us to deal with our material possessions, namely money. God in the Old Testament asks that we give back to Him a tithe (10%) of what He has given to us. Now as Catholic Christians the word "tithe" may not be very familiar to us. It seems that we don't hear that word used much in homilies, mainly because many priests don't like to talk about it. The reason for this hesitancy is that many of us don't tithe ourselves. So we feel a bit uncomfortable talking about and urging our people to do something we're not doing ourselves. I've already admitted that I'm a convert to tithing; and, as any convert, I'm extremely sold on the good of tithing because it is truly being obedient to what God has asked. When we are obedient to Him, He is never outdone in generosity!

To put tithing into an understandable perspective let's go back to the Old Testament. Remember the story of Cain and Abel? I can certainly identify with Cain. He was a very practical person. He would fit very well into our society today. He knew what God asked, a tithe of all he had been given, the first fruits, not what was left over. Now, as we know, Cain was a farmer so his tithe was the first fruits, i.e. the best of his harvest. What was the custom was to burn the first fruits as an offering to God in thanksgiving to God for what He had given them. Cain thought, however, "What's God going to do with the best of the crop? He's not going to eat any of the harvest. I'll offer to Him that which has fallen to the ground which no one will eat anyway." So he gathered all the leftovers and that which was rotten and unfit to eat and burned that as his offering. What happened? The image that the Scripture gives us is that instead of the smoke of the burnt offering rising to the heavens as a sign that the Lord accepted the sacrifice, the smoke stayed on the ground as a sign that the Lord did not accept the offering.

What did Abel do? He was a shepherd and so he took the best lamb from his flock and sacrificed it to the Lord in thanksgiving. His sacrifice, when he immolated it, was accepted by the Lord, the smoke rose to the heavens. The Lord had accepted Abel's tithe. I would bet that you never knew that this story was a story about tithing. Abel was killed by his brother, Cain, because his offering, his first fruits, his tithe, were accepted by God and Cain's wasn't. Abel was obedient and Cain was practical, I mean, disobedient.

Cain had offered God what was left over. I think many times we, with our money, are more like Cain than like Abel. Personally, I used to give God what was left after I took care of what I wanted and needed to do—when I gave Him anything. In fact, for most of my priesthood, I didn't tithe. My reasoning was very simply—and cheaply, I might add—I had given my whole life to God as a priest, certainly I didn't have to give my money also. Was I wrong! Tithing is for everyone no matter how much or how little we earn because tithing is not about **money**. Tithing is all about **our dependence upon God**! That's right. Our **dependence** upon God.

The following is a true story. A priest friend of mine was pastor of a small parish in Canada. Almost all of his parishioners worked for the same company in town. One of his families, who had 18 children, gave more monetarily to the parish than any of the others. One Sunday after Mass my friend asked the father of this large family how he could afford to give what he did. The man simply said, "Father, you've answered your own question. My wife and I have 18 children to provide for and you know where I work so you know approximately how much I earn. I can't afford *not* to tithe. If I didn't tithe I would be telling the Lord that I could take care of my family on my own!" What a fantastic witness for tithing! Truly, hearing that story changed my life. I began to tithe and from that time on I've never worried about money. God is never outdone in generosity! If we really consider what that man with the 18 children said, can any one of us afford not to tithe? Can we really say to God that we can take care of our families or ourselves by our own means? When we tithe we are being obedient to God. When we are obedient to Him then He can be the God of our lives. Yes, even of our finances. Wouldn't it be great never to have to worry about money again! When we tithe that's exactly what happens. Another priest friend of mine comments that God is so good to us that He gives us everything we have and allows us to keep 90% of it for ourselves. Not a bad percentage, if you ask me! Another friend said what would you rather have, 100% without God's blessing or 90% with His blessing? It's our choice as it always is. We either say yes or no to God—even with our money.

When we decide to become obedient to what God asks in regard to our money, we begin to notice how generous God wants to be with us. He is *truly* never outdone in generosity. However, when we are stingy with Him—in any area of our lives, e.g. gifts, talent, money, possessions, relationships—that very stinginess blocks His generosity. You see, it all boils down to this: when we are obedient to Him, when we say yes to Him, when we put Him in the center of our lives, when we allow God to be *the only* God of our lives, then the grace and peace and serenity and joy and security which He longs to give us flood our very senses. When this happens then we experience what being a child of God really is. Being His child, we not only allow Him to take care of us but we depend totally on His doing just that! If we do what God asks He will take care of us. If we don't do what He asks we're telling Him that we can take care of ourselves. Who of us can honestly say that? In obedience there is true freedom! In showing our dependence upon God in every aspect of our lives, including our checkbooks, we shout to the world that God is God and we are not!

The person who shouted that from the very depths of her soul is Our Blessed Mother Mary. Her beautiful *Magnificat* is the song of her dependence upon God and her realization of what that dependence will do for her. Listen as you read the words of her proclamation in Lukes's Gospel, chapter 1, verses 46-55: "My soul magnifies the Lord and my spirit rejoices in God my Savior for He has looked with favor on His lowly servant. From this day all generations will call me blessed for the Almighty has done great things for me and holy is His Name. He has mercy on those who fear Him in every generation. He has shown the strength of His arm, He has scattered the proud in their arrogance, He has cast down the mighty from their thrones, and has lifted up the lowly. He has filled the hungry with good things and the rich He has sent away empty. He has come to the help of His servant Israel for He has remembered His promise of mercy, the promise He made to our fathers, to Abraham and his children forever." In this prayer Mary declared that she knew Who God is and who she is. Using her as our best example of how to say yes to God, one of the things that comes across so strongly about her in the New Testament was, as St. Luke's Gospel relates, "she kept all of these things pondering them in her heart." Pondering means to be quiet and think about what is happening and what is being said. Our Blessed Mother certainly listened to God not only as He spoke to her heart but also as He spoke to her in the events of her daily life. She prayed and thought much more than she spoke. In his gospel St. Luke paints the picture of a very obedient young woman, one who trusted what the Lord was saying to her, one who certainly believed the messenger from Him, and one who was willing to say to that messenger that she really didn't understand what he was saying to her but she said yes because she knew that it was God Who was saying it. What a difference between Mary and all of us! She was completely obedient. We're obedient when we know where the whole thing's going. That's not the obedience God wishes from us. He wishes Mary's obedience from us. The kind of obedience that says, as Mary said, "God asks and so I say yes to it. Wherever my yes leads, He will be there; and so I don't need to worry where my yes will take me." How do we translate that kind of simplicity, that kind of trust in God into our daily life?

First of all we need to try as best as we can to live in the present, not in the past and not in the future. Why? Because God is not in the past. The past is gone! God is not in the future. The future is not here yet. God is only in the present moment. Remember God telling Moses to tell the Israelites that **I AM** sends you. He didn't say tell them I was or I will be sends you. He was in our past when it was our present and He will be in our future when it is our present. Trying to live our lives this way is really a challenge. It's always tempting to look back with either nostalgia or regret. Neither does the present any good. And it's very tempting to follow what the world says and always to look to the future. Again using Mary's example of saying, "Be it done to me according to Your Word," we allow God to take our present so that He can give us our future. But if we are constantly looking back or looking forward we will never experience God, Who is only in the present. And the devil loves us to do that. He wants us to be guilty about our past and worried about our future. When we live our lives like that the devil has us. Our God, on the other hand, takes care of our past in the Sacrament of Reconciliation and gives us our future, if we only learn to live in the present moment. The beautiful prayer of St. Ignatius Loyola is very encouraging in this regard: "Give me only Your love and Your grace. That's enough for me." As you can see, saying yes to God in living in the present moment is a big discipline. In fact it is extremely difficult when the whole world seems to be encouraging us to live the exact opposite. Yet how can we say yes to God about the future, giving it over to Him as Mary did, when we're not even saying yes to Him about the present and when we're regretting what we did in the past?

Maybe one of the best things we could do for ourselves and for our families is to make a resolution not just for a new year but also for the new millennium. This resolution would be: "Y2G"— "Yes to God!"

THE MAIN THING IS TO KEEP
THE MAIN THING THE MAIN THING

What do we believe about God? Now that's an interesting question that maybe we don't reflect enough on. I'm sure that if someone asks you, "Do you believe in God?" you would say, "Yes, I do believe in God!" But how would you explain to him what your belief is? That He is almighty, all-powerful, all loving.... If that was your response you would get an "A" in theology; but, practically speaking, what difference does believing in God make in your life? What difference does believing in Jesus as your Lord and Savior make in your life? Then we move on to the Third Person of the Blessed Trinity, the Holy Spirit. Do you believe in the Holy Spirit? Again, you. would answer, "Yes." But what does the Holy Spirit mean to you? How has the Third Person of the Blessed Trinity affected your life? Do you ever pray to the Holy Spirit? If you were confirmed, what did that mean to you? Did it make you a "soldier of Christ?" Did it make you an "adult member of the Church?" What did you receive when you were confirmed? The gifts and fruits of the Holy Spirit. But what did that mean and how did that make a difference in your life? For 2000 years we as Catholic Christians have said the right things, but talk is cheap unless we follow what we say with how we live. Do people who see us see by the way we live that we believe in God; that we believe that Jesus is our Savior; that the Holy Spirit is truly the Comforter of our soul and the Consoler of our mind and heart, or not? Let me show you why we need to ask ourselves these questions.

First of all, "believing in God." One of the first things we are told about God in Sacred Scripture is that in the beginning God created. Look at the beautiful creation accounts in Genesis. The most beautiful message in those accounts is simply that God loved us so much that He gave us all of creation. God created the world out of love for us. The world is ours. We, however, were created for God. He made us for Himself. What does Scripture say? "Let us make man into Our image. In Our own image let us make him. Male and female let Us make them." The world He created for us;

13

but God created us for Himself. There is a definite order there: the world belongs to us, we belong to God. So what do we believe about God? He created the world out of love for us; He made us in His own image; we belong to Him; and that, if we allow it, He continues to create us in His own image. To put this into a "bumper sticker theology" phrase: "Be patient! God isn't done with me yet!" We really don't believe that, though we use it as an obnoxious excuse for our mistakes instead of glorifying in it as part of the reality of our belonging to Him. He is NOT finished with us yet. He will not be "finished" with us until He calls us home to heaven. Maybe we don't see the implication of what we say, but when we say we believe in God, that He is the all-powerful, the almighty, the One who created the whole world and us in particular, then we don't have to be God. We don't have to know all the answers. When we say, "Well, I'm only human" instead of that being a put-down, it should be an exclamation giving glory to God. I am not a tree. I am not a dog. I am not a rock. I am a human being. God created me for Himself! In that very belonging, in that realization, we acknowledge what the main thing is. And the main thing, as we know, is not a thing at all. The main thing is a Person. The main One. GOD!

The challenge comes in putting what we say we believe into practice. Many times, by the way we live, we are really saying, "I believe in me!" We do this by always trying to be in control, by wanting to have the last word, by always wanting to be "in the know." Because of this we tend to believe that it's all on our shoulders, that the burden is very heavy and the yoke is definitely not easy. This happens when God is not our Center, when we forget to keep the main thing the main thing. Throughout Sacred Scripture God reminds us of the proper order of things: "I will be your God and you will be my people." We quickly forgot that so He sent the prophets to remind us. And what did we do to the prophets for reminding us that God is God and we are not? We ignored them, ran them out of town, or killed them. We didn't like that reminder— and we still don't! The prophet Micah put it very simply for us by saying: "God demands this, and only this, that you act justly, that you love tenderly, and that you walk humbly with your God." How beautiful and how simple! But very difficult to live out! To "act justly" simply means that we don't put ourselves in the number one spot, that we consider the needs of others. To "love tenderly" means that we don't judge others, that we presume the good and not the bad. To "walk humbly with your God" means basically that we are honest with God, that we acknowledge by the way we live that He is God and we are not.

These were the reminders given to us in the Old Testament. How about the ones in the New Testament? What does Jesus tell us about God and our relationship with Him, to help us see that He really is the main thing? Jesus tells us that God is our Father and asks us to call Him "Father" whenever we speak to Him. He wants us to remember that God is not a god distant from us but God is the God close to us, as close as a loving Father. What does Jesus say about God as the "main thing?" How many times in the New Testament do we hear Him saying things like: "What I'm saying is not mine, but His Who sent Me," "The Father and I are one," "I come not to do My own will, but to do the will of Him Who sent Me." Then, when the leaders of the people pressed Him to answer what was the most important, the first, of all the commandments, what did Jesus say? "Love the Lord, your God, with all of your heart, with all of your mind, and with all of your strength." The main thing is to keep the main thing the main thing! The second most important commandment, Jesus said, is like the first: "Love your neighbor as yourself." We can only keep the second only if we keep the first first.

When we proclaim by the way we live that God is our Father, especially when we pray the Our Father, we say some very important things about God and also about ourselves in our relationship to others. First of all, we don't say "my Father," we say "our Father." With that we declare not only that we are not orphans but also that we are not an only child. Many times, however, we act like we are orphaned, that we are all alone and that we have no one to be accountable to. We act like we are the be all and end all of our existence; and, therefore, we need to take care of ourselves and to make things happen! (How often are we told that by our society?) When we act in this way we are simply declaring that we are the main thing. The simple fact is that God is our Father. We belong to Him. We are not orphans. If we will listen, God, our Father, tells us how to live and gives us what we need. In Matthew's Gospel chapters 5,6,and 7, Jesus gives us His Sermon on the Mount. Truly in those three chapters Jesus reveals how much God loves us and how He wants to take care of us. These are the chapters which absolutely changed St. Francis of Assisi's life! "Look at the birds of the air. They do not toil or sow or reap; but your heavenly Father takes care of them. Look at the lilies of the field. Even Solomon in all his splendor was not robed as these. If God takes care of all these little things and makes even the grass beautiful, which dries up tomorrow, how much more will He take care of you? O, you, of little faith! So don't worry over what you are to wear or what you are to eat or what you are to drink. The pagans worry about those things." It seems to me that when we read these beautiful words of Jesus we should be very embarrassed because we do worry about all of these things as if we had to provide for ourselves and our families without God's help. You see, when we worry about those things, we are not keeping the main thing the main thing.

A good litmus test for us to see if we are keeping God first is this. If we find ourselves worrying about family members or finances, then we are trying to take control. I know the world tells us that if you are a mother, worrying about the family is part of your job description; that if you are a father, worrying about finances is part of your job description. All this reminds me of another parable of Jesus'. "There was a man who had many possessions. He said, 'My barns are too small. I will tear them down and build bigger ones so that I can put all my grain into them. Then I can say to myself, "Eat, drink, and be merry! Everything is fine!" But God said to him," You fool, this very day your life will be required of you!" When we don't keep the main thing the main thing, then we act like the man in this parable. When we do keep the main thing the main thing, then God can and does take care of us. With that also come His peace, joy, and contentment.

If we believe what we say we do, then we will trust that God will keep His promises. Because we are His children, He will listen to what we ask and He will give us what we need. To this end we need to follow the example Our Blessed Mother gives us regarding petitionary prayer. Again, going to Sacred Scripture, in John's Gospel, the account of the wedding feast at Cana. The bride and groom ran out of wine at the reception. Mary said to Jesus, "They have no more wine." She simply presented the fact to her Son, knowing that He would take care of the matter. Notice Mary didn't tell Him what to do, how to do it, or when she wanted it done. This is the kind of trust we need to have in God, our Father. When we have this kind of trust, then we are keeping the main thing the main thing.

To keep the main thing the main thing, it might help to look at how some of the saints kept God first in their lives. I would like to begin with two of the most recent uncanonized (without an "St." in front of their names) saints. First, Mother Theresa of Calcutta. She was a Presentation Sister, working as a teacher in a girl's school. Up to that point her life was extraordinarily unspectacular. Extraordinarily unspectacular until she let God do with her what He wanted to do. I'm not saying that she had not already dedicated her life to God as a religious; but, I think, there comes a time in each of our lives, as it did for Mother Teresa, where God gives us the opportunity to truly allow Him to take over. When that happened to her, she abandoned everything and everyone to begin to work with the poorest of the poor. How this was to be accomplished she did not know. All she was certain of was that God had asked her to do this and she had said, "Yes." God took that "Yes" of hers and transformed the way the world looks at the poor. What a great example for us. What was the main thing in her life? Not her Order. Not her work. It was He who called her and she responded wholeheartedly because He was at the center of her life. Her call was a simple one: to quench the thirst of Jesus by working with the poorest of the poor. This was what He asked and this was what she did. No more, no less. As she said so often, "Do little things with great love." Because she kept the main thing the main thing, Mother Teresa never saw a poor person. She never saw a sick person. She never saw a dying person. Whom she always saw was Jesus: poor Jesus, sick Jesus, dying Jesus; and she did the best she could to take care of Him "in the distressing disguise of the poorest of the poor."

The second uncanonized saint for us to consider is Blessed Pope John XXIII. In his spiritual autobiography, *Journal of a Soul*, we see another very simple human being, totally in love with God and trying as best he could to keep God at the center of his life. Pope John's great example for us is his obedience to God and to the Church. In his long service to God in the Church, he never asked for a particular assignment. He always went where he was told. When he was elected Pope he accepted in obedience and trusted that God knew what He was doing. God was the main thing, not Pope John. And when his chief advisors spoke against calling Ecumenical Council, he listened to what God wanted him to do. Had he looked at his own talents and abilities or at the enormous task ahead or even at the consequences instead of keeping his eyes and heart on Jesus, the Second Vatican Council would never have happened!

Looking at any of the lives of the saints, the one thing that they all have in common is that, at some point, they realized who God was and made a conscious decision to turn their lives over to Him. To keep Him as the main thing. To listen to Him above all others, to obey Him, to follow Him, to trust Him, to live for Him alone. For us, I believe, this means to let God "call the shots". To discern what He really wants from us instead of constantly trying to interest Him in all the good we do! But how do we let God "call the shots?"

First, as the psalmist says, we need to "be still and know that I (God) am God." We do this in our private prayer time. When I forget to give the Lord a specific time during the day to be in His Presence, I never get accomplished what I want to get accomplished. I never have enough time. When I do give Him that time, I find that, on those days, I have more than enough time to do what needs to be done. On those days, in taking the time to pray, I am keeping the main thing the main thing—God and my relationship with Him. When we don't set aside time for private prayer then the thing at hand, the presenting crisis, my thoughts, feelings, needs, and desires (even the good ones) become my main concern. How I'm going to have to deal with these things; not how God wants me to deal with them.

Second, we need to slow down. Things that matter the most take time to develop, take time to grow. The quick fix never works! Again, "be still and know that I (God) am God," not "Go berserk and forget that God even exists!" When we keep the main thing the main thing, there will be a peaceful calmness within us because we are certain that God is in control. Things will be taken care of in His time not in ours. What a freedom that gives us!

Third, we need to make use, frequently, of the Sacrament of Reconciliation. When we receive this Sacrament often—I recommend every four to five weeks—we focus on the mercy of God and not on our sins. When we don't receive this Sacrament regularly, we tend either not to think of our sins at all or think that they are too great or too many for God to forgive. When that happens our sin is the main thing and not God and His mercy. Through this Sacrament we remind ourselves that God is more powerful than any sin we commit; and that, through His mercy, He is still loving us and calling us out of our sinfulness. That's what the saints saw. That's what the "saints" in our everyday lives see. That's why there is a difference in the way they live their lives. They have truly come to realize that God is God and they are not. They don't have to know it all or solve it all. They keep the main thing the main thing. That's true holiness.

Fourth, we need to simplify our lives. When we forget that we are not God, we overextend ourselves. We become so busy with so many things that we have time for no one. We need to ask ourselves this question and then, truly, listen for the answer: "What is God really asking me to do?" What is His Will for me? I'm willing to bet that this will be the answer: Put Me at the center of your life! When we do that everything will fall into place. Then we will act justly, love tenderly, and walk humbly with our God. We will not be possessed by our possessions, but will use them for the honor and glory of God and for the benefit of those in need. In simplicity is true freedom!

The end result of keeping the main thing the main thing, keeping God at the center of our lives, realizing that God is God and we are not, will be that we trust Him in everything we do and in everything that happens each day. There's a little plaque in a garden of a convent in Phoenix that says, "Father, I don't understand You but I trust You." What an awesomely humble statement! With that we say, "Father, I may not understand what's going on right now, but I do trust that in all of what's happening You are very much there and in control of the situation. I know that You are God; that You are my Father, and, although I my not understand what's going on right now, I do trust that in all of what's happening You are very much there and in control of the situation. I know that You are God; that You sent Your only Son to save me; that You have given me Your Holy Spirit Who is with me constantly. So, although I don't understand and may never understand this side of heaven, I tell You with as much love as I can muster: 'I trust You.'"

To put into practice all that we have discussed above will take the rest of our lives. We won't be able to just "will" it and it will happen. We'll probably have to start over thousands of times a day. No matter! Whatever we need to do to keep the main thing the main thing we need to do it. Why? First, because God, Himself, asks this; and second, because we will only find true peace if we live this way. Remember, the main thing is to keep the main thing the main thing!!!

DON'T BE NICE, BE CATHOLIC

We are told who Jesus is by all kinds of media and all kinds of people. We read *Time* magazine and we get their view of Jesus. We turn on the religion channel and get their view of who Jesus is. We listen to everyone except Jesus Himself. In fact, we in America and perhaps all over the world have created a "jesus" whom we're very comfortable with; one who doesn't challenge us; one who always understands us—and by "understand" we mean, "agrees with whatever we decide to do and whichever way we decide to live. This is not the real Jesus! This is our made-up version. We have created Him into our image and likeness and have not allowed Him to continue to create us into His image and likeness. Where do we find the real Jesus? Let's go to the New Testament to see what picture Jesus has painted of Himself through the Evangelists.

When I first began using the phrase, "Don't be nice be Catholic!" some people we're really offended. Not that this was a put-down of others who are not Catholic (which it is not); but because most Christians, Catholics included, thought that it was a put-down of Jesus (which it certainly is not!) If we really look at the Jesus in the New Testament, we see that He wasn't nice. Had He been nice He would never have been crucified! He would have always told everyone exactly what they wanted to hear instead of what they needed to hear, the Truth of God! In other words, Jesus was not politically correct. Jesus was not nice! He was kind, compassionate, merciful, loving, forgiving, and, most of all, He was truthful. In fact, Jesus was and is the Truth of God personified. As He spoke and lived the truth of God, His Father, He challenged everyone, especially the people who thought they had it all together. That is why He was crucified. He always told the truth. Allow me to cite two examples from the Gospels. First, remember the story of Jesus walking along and three people approaching Him. One said I will follow wherever You go. Jesus replied, "The birds of the air have nests, the foxes have dens, but the Son of Man has nowhere to lay his head." In other words, you don't know what you're asking. To the next one Jesus said, "Follow me." This one replied, I will follow you but first I have to bury my father. Jesus answered, "Let the dead bury their dead!" The third one said, I will follow you but I need to go and tell my family good-bye. Jesus replied, "The person who puts his hand to the plow and then turns back is not fit for the reign of God." Those were not "nice" answers, but they were true. The last two statements Jesus made were simply saying that, when God calls, we need to answer and let Him take care of everything else. The second story is the one about the woman caught in adultery. Remember that one? The leaders of the people dragged a woman, who had been caught in the very act, to Jesus and asked Him what needed to be done with her. They said, Moses prescribed that such a one be stoned to death, what do you say, Jesus? He bent down and began tracing in the sand with His finger until He had everyone's attention. Then He stood up and said, "Let him who is without sin caste the first stone." Then He bent down again, giving them all time to think. What happened next? As Scripture says, "They all began to leave, beginning with the oldest. Jesus then stood up and, looking at the woman said, "Doesn't anyone condemn you?" "No one, Lord!" was her answer. Jesus replied, "Neither do I condemn you. Go in peace." Now, had He stopped right there, we'd say, "What a nice Jesus!" He put the bad guys in their place and made the woman feel good. But we know that's not what He did. How did He end the conversation with the adulterous woman? He said, in no uncertain terms, "Go and sin no more!" Don't do that again! That wasn't nice. That, perhaps, was not what she wanted to hear; but that was what she needed to hear. That was the truth!!

This is the kind of Jesus whom we say we follow, whom we claim as Lord and Savior. This is the real Jesus, who stands on and for the truth because He is the Truth. He came into the world, which had forgotten what the truth was. He began telling the truth; and it got Him crucified, didn't it? Where does that leave us? Because of the world we live in and because we've allowed it to tell us who Jesus is and, really, what the truth is and how to live, we want to be nice. We don't want to offend anyone. We are taught by this world of ours that the greatest virtue is being politically correct. And we, yes, even we who say we follow Jesus, buy into this political correctness. Even we who call ourselves Catholic want to be nice because we want to be accepted. If we are truly followers of Jesus we will never really be accepted because Jesus wasn't. Look around! The only Church that is not politically correct is the Catholic Church. The Catholic Church has never been and never will be politically correct. It can't be because Jesus Himself founded it!

We need to follow Jesus in living and speaking His truth. Yet, we are so influenced by our politically correct society that we waffle on almost everything. The old saying: "If you don't stand for something you'll fall for everything," really fits the way we live our lives these days. How many times have we heard or said something like this: "It's my belief, but I certainly wouldn't want to impose my belief on you." We want to be accepted at all costs, even if the "cost" is giving up the truth. The truth is if we follow Jesus, we will never be accepted by the "world" because it never accepted Him. Our society now accepts a watered-down version of Jesus whom it has made into a "nice guy" who doesn't make anyone feel uncomfortable. In fact there is a whole societal "Christianity" which I call the Great American Christian Heresy. This kind of Christianity declares that if you believe in the Lord Jesus as your Savior you will never ever again be ugly or poor or sick! The "Jesus" whom this heresy proclaims is not the Jesus found in the New Testament. This politically correct Jesus makes no one feel uncomfortable. We can believe in this politically correct Jesus and do whatever we want to do, say whatever we want to say, and believe whatever we want to believe as long as we don't make anyone feel uncomfortable. With this kind of Jesus the truth is whatever we want it to be.

The Jesus of the New Testament spoke only the truth of God; there is no other truth! It was because of this that He was nailed to a cross. If we follow Him in speaking and living the truth of God we might not be nailed to a cross, but we will be "nailed" by society. We will be mocked, criticized, looked down upon. We will be called be-nighted, prudish, and the worst of all, politically incorrect! This will not be pleasant for us. We will have to overcome the fear of making people uncomfortable as we live and speak God's truth. Jesus did not set out to make people feel uncomfortable. He set out to speak the truth of His Father without watering it down. That made people uncomfortable. They didn't want to hear it. That got Him crucified and us redeemed!

So, which Jesus are we following? The Jesus of the Great American Christian Heresy or the Jesus of the New Testament? If we feel comfortable every time we come to Mass, we're not following the real Jesus. We should feel comforted not comfortable because the Scripture should challenge the very socks off of us. If it doesn't we're not really listening. In my opinion, that's why Jesus gave us the Eucharist. He knew that following what we read in the Sacred Scriptures, trying to live and speak the truth of God would be very difficult to do as we are trying to be "in" the world and not "of" the world. The Scripture challenges us and the Eucharist strengthens us to live it out. We need to go back into the New Testament and read again about this Jesus. When was the last time you sat quietly with your Bible in hand and really read it? Really let the Word of God, not just the words, sink into your heart? Maybe that's why we're so quick to follow the politically correct Jesus. We don't really take the time to get to know the real One! I believe that we Catholic Christians don't appreciate what we have. This Bible is *our* book! We put the Old Testament together and wrote the New Testament. Sometimes we forget that. So I challenge you to take your Bible and read it, consume it, let this Living Word of God sink again into your very soul! If this is a bit daunting, I suggest that you begin with the Gospel of Luke. Listen to what this Evangelist says about Jesus. Look at Who this God-Man is. How this Messiah acted. This is the Jesus who saved us. This is the Jesus we say we follow. As we see this real Jesus we're going to have to re-examine whether we want to follow Him or not. It is much easier to follow the jesus that our world accepts than to follow the One Who comes to life in the Gospels. Perhaps we'll have to admit that we don't want to follow the real Jesus. However, if, as we allow the Word of God to take hold of our hearts, we recommit ourselves to follow Him wherever He leads then we will need most likely to give up being "nice." For some that will be very difficult. For others it will mean changing an attitude which they've lived with most of their lives; and for all of us it will necessitate begging the real Jesus for grace to make this change in our lives.

If we are Catholic we also have another wonderful resource in not only learning about the real Jesus but also learning how to follow Him as we live in our society. This resource is the 2,000 years of lived and living faith in Jesus, which we call Tradition. For us Catholic Christians there are two sources of public revelation which God has given to us, first, Tradition, and second, the Sacred Scripture. I say, "first, Tradition," because our lived faith as a community preceded our writing it down, Sacred Scripture. And all through the centuries the Church, our faith community, has given us insights as to how we live out this faith, which we have in Jesus. As members of the Catholic Christian church we realize that there is objective truth, given us by God Our Father through Jesus, His Son, and Our Redeemer, in the Sacred Scripture; and that it is through this Church, which Jesus Himself founded on the Rock of Peter, that this objective truth is revealed. This Truth does not and will not and cannot change no matter what society says or does. What a great grace that is for us! We belong to *the* Church, which has been graced with the fullness of the Truth of God. We don't have to keep re-inventing the truth. We have been given the Truth and all we have to do is apply it to our lives; and even then, because of our Tradition, we are also given insights about how best to apply this objective truth in any particular situation in which we find ourselves. Grace upon grace! How blessed we are!

As Catholic Christians the blessings keep on multiplying. Not only do we have the Sacred Scriptures but we also have our lived Tradition written down for us, now most recently in the New Catechism of the Catholic Church. In this book we have elucidated for us not only what we believe but also why we believe what we believe—and where it came from—and also how to live this belief out in this day and age. In addition to the New Catechism we have all of the writings down through the centuries of the Church Fathers, the Councils, and all of the papal encyclicals. All of these make up the teaching Magisterium of the Church. Again, with all of these aids given to us, helping us in each age to live and speak the Truth of God, we don't have to keep re-inventing the wheel. We simply apply what we have always believed as Church to what is happening today. This is simple but not always easy. That's where prayerful discernment enters in. Again, how blessed we are. We can always go to one of the saints, our brothers and sisters already in heaven, and read their autobiography or a biography written about them to see how they handled the various situations they were confronted with as they tried to live and speak the Truth of God in their lives. As we read accounts of their lives and the challenges they faced in being true to Our Lord, we realize that in fact there is nothing new under the sun. What comfort that can give us—and what great perspective.

Many times we are challenged in ways which seem insurmountable. We are confronted with decisions to be made which, we believe, would strain the wisdom of King Solomon. When these things happen we can be assured that we don't have to face them on our own. We are grounded in the Word of God in Sacred Scripture, we are members of the Church, founded by Jesus Himself, and, because of that, we have the benefit of 2,000 years of lived faith experience of millions of people who lived out their belief in this Jesus and who even gave lives willingly for this lived belief. We are firmly rooted because of this faith and firmly grounded by this faith community to withstand anything "the world, the flesh, or the devil" may throw at us. We stand humbly and gratefully on the shoulders of these men and women who were giants of the Faith. There is nothing we have to fear! Because we are Catholic Christian there is no such thing as a problem. In fact, we need to strike that word from our vocabulary. Because of our faith there are only challenges to meet, not problems to solve. There can only be problems when God is not with us; and, because of our Baptism, God is *always* with us! This may seem like an insignificant distinction but it's not. The devil loves to tempt us into believing that life consists of one problem after another. When this happens then our lives become very burdensome and the load becomes very heavy. The reality is that life does present us with challenge after challenge; but, because of our faith, we can meet each of these challenges with strength and grace and resilience. Again, how blessed we are!

Our challenge is to live and speak the Truth of Jesus as best we can all the time; to avoid the temptation to be "nice," to be politically correct; and to rely on the strength of the Sacred Scripture and Tradition handed down to us by the Catholic Church. In living and speaking this way, we will show to anyone who sees us the freedom that can also be theirs. The truth will set us free! Don't be nice, be Catholic!!

Until He Comes Again

THE CROSS OF HOLINESS

When I used to think of crosses, as in "we must carry our cross," I used to picture suffering, pain, and things that would cause me some kind of discomfort. The older we all become, however, and the more aches and pains we have, I think we realize that these aches and pains, both physical and emotional, are just part of that "cross" we've been asked to carry. Especially for us, who are followers of Our Lord Jesus, the real cross we are asked to carry everyday is the cross of being holy. This cross of holiness is what I want to reflect upon with you. I am almost positive that when I called holiness a cross, a question mark formed in your mind. I say that I am fairly certain that was your reaction because that was my reaction also the first time I really considered this possibility. What triggered this whole idea was something I heard Mother Teresa of Calcutta say in response to the question: "How does it feel being a living saint?" which a reporter asked her at a press conference when she visited Phoenix in 1989. She looked at the man and simply replied, "Holiness is not the privilege of the few, but the simple duty of each of us." Let me assure you; there weren't many questions after that! Ever since that afternoon, that simple statement of fact continues to challenge me. It really is that simple. Holiness is our duty, our task. It is what we are put on earth to achieve; and it is the fruit of the redemption won for each of us—and all of us—by the Suffering, Death, and Resurrection of Our Lord Jesus. Holiness is ours for the having. However, as is the case with most things of real value, holiness doesn't just happen. It takes work and time—really, the rest of our lives. When we wake up dead someday and stand before the Lord, it will be too late to work on our holiness. We need to remember that we won't be saints in heaven unless we're saints first here on earth!

So, if holiness is our simple duty, and I for one am not going to disagree with Mother Teresa, how do we "become" holy? And, why would this holiness be a cross? Fasten your seat belts; you may be in for the ride of your life. The one which will take us all from here to eternity!

It seems to me that most of us don't give much thought to being holy. Oh, most of us, especially if we are Catholic, go to Mass on Sundays and Holy Days. We probably pray our morning and night prayers when we think of it and when we're not too tired. We try to keep most of the Commandments most of the time. But how often have we really dedicated some goodly amount of time, concentrating on how we can become holier—or just holy. We get so wrapped up in our daily lives and responsibilities of family and job and community that we don't give much thought, if any, to our main responsibility, becoming holy, which in turn will bring us to heaven. (Remember? That's why God made us: "to know, love, and serve Him in this world so that we can be happy with Him in the next.") When we do take the time to think about how to become holy we realize that because of what Jesus did for us on the cross, through this Redeeming Action of His, we have been given this inestimable opportunity to go to heaven. Again, it is ours for the taking. What holds us back? For starters, human respect. We don't want to come across as "holier than thou." How many times have we said: "I'm no saint" or "What do you think I am a saint or something?" Do we realize that when we make comments like these what we're really saying is: "Jesus, your death on the cross has meant nothing to me. It has made no difference in my life. The way I live is no different from the way everyone else lives their lives—even those who have never heard of you." We don't want to stand out or draw attention to ourselves. See where holiness is a cross in this area of our lives? It is my opinion that we don't have to look for crosses in our life. All we have to do is to try to live each day as if Jesus' Passion, Death, and Resurrection really means everything to us and really makes a difference in the *way* we live, in the *way* we speak, and in the *way* we love. Try this cross on for size!

Secondly, I think we equate being holy with being perfect. So, as we begin to realize that being perfect is something that, most likely, will not happen for us, we also then believe that being holy is also something that is out of our reach. This is a very wrong assumption. Being perfect and being holy are two different things. Our Church in one of the greatest feasts gives one of the greatest examples of this difference to us in our liturgical year. The Feast I'm referring to is celebrated on the Sunday after Christmas, the

Feast of the Holy Family. Notice the Church didn't call it the Feast of the Perfect Family. The Church holds Joseph, Mary, and Jesus up to us as the *Holy* Family, because, if we look at them as their society did, they weren't "perfect." Mary became pregnant before she was married. Joseph didn't really follow the accepted custom of "putting her away quietly." He married her. They had only the one child, which was considered an abnormality, even a curse, because the Jewish people at that time, at least, considered having many children not only a blessing but as *the* way of having some kind of immortality by living on through their children. So, as far as their society went, they were not the example of the perfect, or even typical, Jewish family. They didn't try to be the perfect family. They tried to be the holy family. They tried and succeeded to follow exactly what God, the Father, asked of them—and so they were holy.

How about our families and us? It is very easy to be swept up in letting our society dictate what it is to be the perfect American family. We need to have 2.5 children; 2 cars, one of them preferably a mini-van or SUV, until the children get their driver's license and then each of them need a car, again, preferably a newer model; the children need to go to the proper preschool so that they can get into the proper grade school so they can get into the proper college-prep high school so they can get into the proper university so that they will have the proper contacts to get in the right position to advance their careers so that they will be able to begin this same cycle with their spouse and children. Wow! No wonder Prozac has become our friend! No wonder that our children feel so much pressure to succeed that they too become stressed out! When was the last time we sat down to dinner with all our family members present? When was the last time we took the time to enjoy each other's company? I'm not against, and, more importantly, neither is God, having children involved in soccer, or baseball, or football, or cheerleading, or dance, or kung-fu; but, if these things take precedence over our being a family, then something is wrong. Maybe the question to ask when we are tempted to get so involved in what society is encouraging us to do is: "Is this (insert the activity, the thing, the relationship, the career of the moment) going to bring me closer to heaven?" Perhaps, the better question would be: "Is this (again insert the activity, thing, relationship, career) leading me further from heaven?" As you know it is not easy living as a holy family, when society wants—and expects—us to be a perfect family! We need to realize that we will never be the perfect family, but we *can* be a holy family. What do we need to do to make this happen? Thought you'd never ask! We begin with ourselves, not our families. As we know from every psychology book and from every talk-show host on radio and television, the only one we can change is ourselves. So that's where we begin. However, we need to remember that when it comes to anything that pertains to our relationship with God, it is not what we do but what we allow God to do for us. He is the One to make us holy; not ourselves. We don't do it. God does! Through His Son, Jesus, God tells us how we need to prepare ourselves for Him to make us holy. Remember what Jesus said to the man who asked Him what was the most important, the first commandment? He said, "Love the Lord your God with all your heart with all your soul with all your mind and with all your strength." And we show God that we love *Him* by loving our neighbor as ourselves. These are not new to us, are they? Of course not. Yet are we putting them into practice? If we were, we would be well on our way to holiness. Maybe St. Paul's words to the people of Rome will give us the encouragement we need to pick up this cross of holiness: "Do not conform yourselves to this age but be transformed by the renewal of your mind, so that you may judge what is God's will, what is good, pleasing and perfect."

Beginning to live a life of holiness will necessitate our not conforming to "this age." This means simply that we stop listening to what the world says is important and valuable and begin to really listen to what God tells us is important and valuable. We hear this as we read His Word both in the Old and New Testament. We hear this in the quiet of our prayer time. We hear this as we celebrate Holy Mass. We hear this as God speaks to us through the teaching of the Church. As we listen God will lead us ever closer to Him. It isn't easy to listen to Him, especially when so many are listening to what the world says. Is this a cross? Certainly.

Another part of this holiness cross is obedience. As we are all aware, especially in our own society today, people don't even know how to spell the word obedience, let alone practice it. It seems that the prevailing attitude is one of "who says?" or "no one tells me what to do." For us who follow Christ our attitude must be like His, as St. Paul says in his letter to the Philippians. His attitude was one of humility and obedience, "even to death, death on a cross." Our obedience to God and to the Church may not cause our physical death, but it will require us to die to our selfishness and the real temptation to do everything "my way." Is this a cross? Certainly.

Next, there is the matter of forgiveness. This is definitely part of the cross we are asked to carry on the path to holiness. Forgiveness, also, is foreign to the world in which we live. Our world says, "Don't get mad, get even." This doesn't square not only with what God has asked of us; but it doesn't go along with the example which Jesus gave us through His parables and in His own life. "Father, forgive them for they know not what they do," is a far cry from how we are encouraged to presume the bad in everyone instead of the good. Will this make us stand out in our society? Yes. Will forgiveness be difficult and sometimes, seemingly, impossible? Yes. Is forgiveness a cross? Certainly. This part of the cross of holiness will be impossible for us to carry without surrendering to God, without admitting to Him our helplessness in this area. With this, then, we come to the most difficult part of this cross: living in the present moment.

Living in the present moment may not seem to be much of a cross. But what this means is that we give up our past and our future to the Lord. That we learn from our past, that we ask forgiveness and healing, and that we move on. That we don't live in the past and wallow in regret or guilt, which is so common with so many people and so encouraged by our society. That we don't worry about our future or the future of our family or of our world. That we trust in the loving Providence of Our Heavenly Father, believing that, no matter what happens, He is there in the midst of it all and will take care of us and everyone and everything. Will this set us apart from our contemporaries? Yes. Is this a cross? Certainly!

Our Lord's command to "take up your cross, daily, and follow Me" is just that, a command. This is the only way to live with Him forever in heaven. This command should also give us encouragement because of the "daily." We'll most likely drop our cross often. It's not easy to be holy. But no matter how often we drop it, the important thing for us and to Our Lord is that we pick it up again and move forward. He gave us the example in His own way of the Cross. We won't become holy overnight. Holiness will take our whole life. It will require complete dependence upon God. It will ask of us to constantly look upon the mercy of God instead of looking at our sinfulness. To not be discouraged by our faults and failings, when we don't live in a holy way, but to be always willing to seek forgiveness from others and from God. To carry the cross of holiness is not for the faint of heart! Maybe that's why there are so few saints. Our Lord wouldn't ask the impossible of us. With all things are possible—even us becoming saints!! This is our task, our "simple duty." And as we allow Our Lord to lead us down this path of holiness we will see a difference in those around us and especially in our families. We know that we lead by example better than edict. Jesus has given us the example. We, in turn give that example to others. St. Francis of Assisi captured this, I think, when he said, "I preach the Gospel and sometimes I use words." A line from one of the songs of the late Rich Mullins, a great contemporary Christian musician, I hope will help you carry your cross of holiness as it helps me carry mine: "A saint is just a sinner who falls down and gets up."

JESUS LOOKS AT THE TEN COMMANDMENTS

The most basic thing we need to do until Jesus comes again is keep the commandments given to us by God, Our Father, through Moses on Mount Sinai. Let me list them as a point of reference as we take a look at how Jesus has asked us to observe them:

I.   I am the Lord, thy God, thou shalt not have strange gods before Me.
II.   Thou shalt not take the Name of the Lord, thy God, in vain.
III. Remember, thou, to keep holy the Sabbath.
IV.   Honor thy father and thy mother.
V.   Thou shalt not kill.
VI.   Thou shalt not commit adultery.
VII. Thou shalt not steal.
VIII. Thou shalt not bear false witness against thy neighbor.
IX.   Thou shalt not covet thy neighbor's wife.
X.   Thou shalt not covet thy neighbor's goods.

This is quite a list! The reason, of course, that God so graciously gave us these commandments was, not to cramp our lifestyle as so many in our society believe, but to help us live here on earth in peace and harmony with one another so that we might live forever with Him in heaven. These are truly commandments, not suggestions as others today would have us believe; and they are as relevant and as applicable today as they were when God first gave them to us. They have not and will not go out of style!

What a difference there is between the way God makes a list and the way we do. Usually, when we make a "to do" list we don't necessarily put the things in order. We put down the first thing that comes to our minds. When God makes a list He certainly prioritizes, having the list go from the most important on down. So when we look at the Ten Commandments, the first is the most important followed by the second and third and so forth. Isn't it interesting that most of us, especially us Catholics and especially when we are preparing for the Sacrament of Reconciliation (i.e. Confession, for those of us over 55!), go immediately to Commandment Six. If we're "clean" with that one, we hardly have anything to confess! Did you ever stop to think that #6 didn't even make it into the top five!! Have we ever confessed breaking Commandment #1? That's the most important one. Have we ever broken it? How about the second and the third? The first three commandments deal with our relationship with God Himself. The last seven deal with how we relate with our fellow human beings.

So before we too quickly say "no" to having never broken the First Commandment and make excuses for "bending" the Second and Third, we really need to take a closer look at what is involved in keeping each of the Ten Commandments. To begin with, we who call ourselves followers of Jesus Christ need to realize that He raised the bar, so to speak, when it comes to observing the commandments. Remember that section in Matthew's Gospel, Chapter 5, where He started saying, " You have heard it said…but I say to you?" He "fleshed out" the commandments, showing us what it truly means to live not only the letter but also the spirit of the Law. Let us begin.

FIRST COMMANDMENT:
I AM THE LORD, THY GOD, THOU SHALT NOT HAVE STRANGE GODS BEFORE ME.

This is obviously a reference to idolatry. People at that time, other than the Israelites, worshiped many gods, some other their own making and some from nature itself, i.e. sun, moon, wind, fire, and even mother earth. This commandment certainly doesn't apply to us enlightened people of the 21st century, does it? I certainly does! If we're not worshiping the gods of the new age movement or the earth or the other elements of the universe, we're worshiping power or money or sex or…. I think you understand. This commandment applies just as much to us now than it did when it was first given.

As I said previously, I would be willing to bet that the majority of us have never ever confessed breaking the First Commandment. However, this is the one commandment we break more than any of the other nine. Whenever we put someone or something in God's place we're breaking this commandment. How do we do this? Let me give you a rule of thumb or litmus test to use to see when you are breaking commandment number one. Whoever or whatever you are worried about, are anxious about, or are fixated on—that person or that thing is really your god. But, you say, the very definition of being a mom or dad is to worry about the children or health or finances. Actually, not!! Being a parent means that you gratefully accept the gift of your children and trust that the Lord will help you take care of them. I believe that the main reason most of us tend to break this commandment is that we listen to what the world says we need to do to take care of our families or ourselves. When we listen to the world through our society we know that we will never be thin or rich enough personally; that we will spend most of our time "keeping up with the Jones," and never be able to give our children all the things that we are told by Madison Ave. we need to give them. So, both parents work maybe two or three jobs just to make ends meet—the "ends" that society dictates need to be met if we are to be considered good parents and successful individuals. Talk about worry or anxiety. Talk about pressure. Wow! No wonder these kinds of things are on our mind all the time. No wonder they become *the* focus of our lives. They become our gods; and we do all in our power to serve them. We worship on the altars of greed and prosperity, of designer clothing and snob appeal, of society pages and self-respect. These things can so easily become our idols. It is really scary how quickly we can be sucked into the "values" the world tells us are so important and the "standards" by which we are to judge our worth and success as human beings. Who really is your God? We need to truly examine our lives as well as our consciences in this area, and, perhaps, very humbly admit that this first of the commandments is the one we break most of the time. If this is the case, then we need to include the ways we have allowed people or things to take the place of God in our lives the next time we go to the Sacrament of Reconciliation.

SECOND COMMANDMENT:
THOU SHALT NOT TAKE THE NAME OF THE LORD,
THY GOD, IN VAIN.

This second of the three commandments, which pertain to our relationship with God, has to with the way we hold His Name in reverence. Do we give Him honor and glory as we use His sacred Name? In the days of the Old Testament, the Israelites could not even say the name of God. They would call Him God of the universe, God of our fathers, but, in fact, there was no name for God. Remember when Moses asked God, Who had appeared to him in the burning bush and ask him to go to Egypt to ask Pharaoh to let the Israelites leave that country to go to the Promised Land, whom shall I tell them sent me? What was God's answer? Tell them "I AM" sent you. From the very beginning God's holy name was to be used only with tremendous reverence and awe.

Jesus gave us the Name by which we are to address the Almighty, the All-Powerful, the All-Knowing God. The One Who is Who was and Who is to come. Jesus said to call God Our Father. What a revelation! What a gift! To think that we are to refer to the Creator of the universe as our Father. If we really give this some thought, it is really overpowering. Then we reflect upon how flippantly we sometimes use His Holy Name. We need to be profoundly ashamed and embarrassed. We use The Name of God or the name of Our Blessed Mother or the saints to damn someone or something; to swear to someone or something; to curse someone or something; or to simply express our frustration or anger. Truly a blasphemy! Oh, I know that many times we don't even think about what we're saying; but that's it, isn't it. We don't think— and we should—before we open our mouths. When we use the Holy Name of God or of Our Blessed Mother Mary or of one of the saints, we need to be giving honor and glory to His Name. We need to always use His Name with reverential awe. Perhaps we need to ask God to help us to be more silent and to reflect before we say anything. The fact is we use the Name of God in the wrong way most of the time. This misuse has become a bad habit. This misuse also gives scandal, especially to those who know we are

Catholic, whether we realize it or not; and it also gives bad example, especially to our children. We need to truly examine how we have used and are using the Name of God and all the saints in our daily lives; and, if we have been misusing them, then we need to bring this misuse to the healing and forgiving power of Reconciliation.

THIRD COMMANDMENT:
REMEMBER, THOU, TO KEEP HOLY THE SABBATH.

The third and last of the commandments which has to do with our relationship with God pertains to our worshiping Him as a community. This one deals with public prayer and with how we honor Him on His day. When this commandment was given, the Lord's Day was the Sabbath, the last day of the week. The day for rest for the Israelites from their work and a day dedicated to public prayer and worship of God, the Lord of the Sabbath. It was to be a holy day, one set aside for God and for family. With the Resurrection of Jesus on the first day of the week, the early followers of Jesus began to keep this day also holy, as the Lord's Day. When they were expelled from the synagogues and began to be persecuted for their belief in Jesus as the Messiah, the Lord's Day became the first day of the week, Sunday. So, for us, the question is, how do we keep holy the Lord's Day? How do we observe Sunday as a day of worship and rest? Is it different from the other days of the week for us, or not? If not, why not?

One of the gifts of the Second Vatican Council was that we were given the privilege of being able to celebrate a vigil Mass for every Sunday and Holy Day of Obligation. This means that we can fulfill our Sunday or Holy Day obligation of celebrating Holy Mass on Saturday evening. This special dispensation was given specifically for the benefit of those who could not attend Mass on Sunday or on a Holy Day because of work or some other exceptional circumstance. This is really a gift to us—a gift that many misuse. In many parishes one of the most highly attended Masses is the Saturday evening vigil. Is the reason for this that so many of the parishioners work on Sunday or are going to be traveling? I don't think so. For many the reason for going to Mass on Saturday evening is to "get it (the Holy Mass) out of the way so that they can have all of Sunday for themselves." Sunday is <u>not</u> our day! Sunday is *God's* day! Many people also go to the earliest Mass on Sunday for the same reason. This is the wrong reason! We should not "get it out of the way," or "fit it in to our schedule." Mass on Sunday should be the center of that holy day. We should fit what we do on Sunday around Holy Mass, not the other way around. To observe this Third Commandment faithfully we should not do any kind of work on Sunday, which we could have done or should have done on the other six days. Now, obviously, if a person works six days a week, maybe the only day they can do the laundry, or clean the house, or mow the yard, or shop is Sunday. If that's the case, then they need to do what they have to do. I dare say, though, that for the majority of us, most of the things we find ourselves doing, work wise, on Sundays, we could do any other day of the week. Sundays are for worshipping God as a community and resting and relaxing with friends and family, giving honor and glory to God as we do these things. So the question is: Do we keep holy the Lord's Day or is it just another day of the week, or, perhaps worse, is it *our* day? If we have been misusing Sundays then we need to humbly ask forgiveness and absolution in our next trip to the confessional.

FOURTH COMMANDMENT:
HONOR THY FATHER AND MOTHER.

With the Fourth Commandment we are shown by God how we are to relate to each other. It is not insignificant that the first commandment in this second part of the Decalogue has to do with the first relationship that any of us has, that of our family. Again, from the very first book of the Old Testament, Genesis, we are told that this (to live as a family) is "why a man forsakes his mother and a woman leaves her home…and the two become one." The basic relationship, which exists between parent and child, is the most critical and formative that any of us has in our lives. All through the Old Testament, in book after book there is reference after reference about the blessings, which come from having children and from honoring and taking care of parents. The common mistake most adults make as we go down the commandments as we examine our consciences is that when we come to number four we dismiss it because we are not children anymore and most of us are willing to take care of our aging parents as best we can. Others tend to avoid looking at this commandment because of an irreparable something that happened in their relationship with their parents. Both of these reactions miss the mark. Perhaps in the second scenario mentioned the only thing, and the best thing, to be done is simply thank God for the gift of life given to them through their parents and to keep their distance, offering the whole relationship to God for His healing and mercy.

The majority of us adults fit into that first category. We think this commandment applies to our children but not to us. If that's our thinking we are mistaken. This commandment deals with obedience and respect for proper authority. If that's the case, and it is, the question we need to ask ourselves is how obedient and respectful are we of proper, lawful, authority? How obedient and respectful are we to those people both civil and ecclesiastical (state and Church) whom God has put in authority over us? Ah, there's the rub! Perhaps we have succumbed to the all-American attitude of "Who says?" or of "Who are you to tell me what to do," or of "Nobody tells me what I should or shouldn't do!" If this is our attitude, then we are breaking the Fourth Commandment.

I don't know if you have ever thought of this or not, but how can we expect and demand obedience from our children if they don't see us as obedient ourselves. The basic question needs to be, "To whom are we obedient?" Have you ever heard a young teenager say something like, I can hardly wait to become an adult because then I can do whatever I want and nobody will tell me what to do? Where do the teens get that idea? Obviously, from watching the example which we adults give them. What kind of example of respect and obedience do we give to all of our young people, especially to our own children, when right in front of them we criticize or even ridicule civil or Church authorities. In doing that, don't we give our young people the green light to criticize and ridicule us? When they see us breaking civil or church laws or being disobedient to what we've been asked to do by state or Church, should we be surprised or upset when our children refuse to obey us? When we lie to those who have been placed in authority over us, should we be surprised when our children lie to us?

As you can see, there is much involved in this commandment, which appears to be only for children. In fact, as we examine our consciences with regard to the Fourth Commandment, it may afford us a great opportunity to do some real soul-searching about what we need to ask God for healing in this area of obedience and respect of proper authority. We need to remember that obedience is truly the key to our salvation. Again, didn't Our Lord give us *the* example of how we need to live, by, as St. Paul says in his letter to the Philippians, Chapter 2, "becoming obedient to death, even death on a cross." And the reward for our obedience will be the same as God, Our Father, gave to His only Son—again Paul's letter to the Philippians—"because of this (obedience) He made His name above all names. That at the mention of His name every knee in heaven and on the earth and below the earth must bend and proclaim to the glory of God that Jesus Christ is Lord."

FIFTH COMMANDMENT:
THOU SHALT NOT KILL.

From the basic familial relationship of honor and respect covered in the Fourth Commandment, the Fifth Commandment deals with the most fundamental right we have as human beings, the prohibition against taking the life of another. It's interesting to note that the second sin recorded in the Old Testament, after the first sin, which was disobedience, is fratricide, Cain taking the life of his brother, Abel. Truly, this commandment, as do all the others, upholds our basic rights which are given to us by our Creator. The intent of this commandment is obvious, taking the life of any human being is gravely wrong. It is also obvious in our society today that human life has become devalued; abortion and euthanasia are gruesome examples of this. Human life is cheap and expendable. The debate continues regarding the moral validity of war and capital punishment. (I suggest reading Pope John Paul II's encyclical, "The Gospel of Life," for some phenomenal insights into this whole subject.)

The majority of us most likely are not guilty of taking someone's life. There is, however, another dimension of this commandment which we need to consider. This is the matter of how we take care of ourselves physically and emotionally. Are we trying to live a healthy life? Do we eat the proper food so that our bodies get the correct nourishment they need to grow and to fight off disease? Do we exercise our bodies so that they remain strong and, again, so that they can ward off sickness? How concerned are we about our emotional health? Do we continue to put ourselves in situations which are emotionally unhealthy or stressful? Granted these situations sometimes arise, but there is a difference when these become a lifestyle. Our bodies are the temples of the Holy Spirit. In fact they don't belong to us; they belong to God, Who created them. How do we take care of this gift? Do we continue to feed and to give our mind and intellect the stimulation they need to keep growing? These, too, are gifts from God. How are we taking care of them? Let me say that I am not encouraging any of us to join the "cult" of the body, which is constantly being promoted by Madison Ave. What I am simply presenting is a reminder of the obligation each of us has to care for the body and mind and intellect, which have been given to us by God.

So, as we examine our consciences through the lens of the Fifth Commandment, we may need to seek forgiveness from God, the Giver of all life, for the times when we have neglected to proper care, not only of the lives of others, but also of our own life.

SIXTH COMMANDMENT:
THOU SHALT NOT COMMITT ADULTERY.

The Sixth Commandment basically prohibits having sexual intercourse with another person who is not our spouse as well as sexual intercourse between people who are not married. As we look at this commandment we need to be aware, first of all, of the beautiful gift of our sexuality and how precious a gift it is in the sight of

God, Who created it. It is through this wonderful gift that we, human beings, co-operate with God, Himself, in the process of creation. It is through the gift of sexual intercourse of husband and wife in the Sacrament of Marriage that we participate in the very life of God and of the Holy Trinity! No wonder the devil wants to destroy marriage and wants to degrade and trivialize our sexuality. It certainly is apparent that he has had his way in our society. So, although some would say that this commandment above all the others has become irrelevant today, the fact is that following this commandment is very likely the only way in which we can turn our society around. The misuse of sexuality is epidemic. It is an epidemic, which could literally kill us. Yet we claim enlightenment in this whole area and state very emphatically that we know what's good for us—implying that God doesn't. Again, the fact is that this commandment as the others is given to us not to cramp out style, but to help us have a full and joyful life!

The unfortunate thing is that we have been so brainwashed by what the world says about sexuality that we begin to believe what is not true. Especially in the area of sexuality the attitude which permeates our lives is that we are the ones who make the judgment about its meaning about its use and about its value—as if we were the creators and owners of this gift. When we use sexuality in whatever way we deem right and acceptable what we're saying is that God doesn't know what He's talking about, or, worse yet but most likely more accurate, we don't care what God is saying, we'll do what we want whenever we want with whomever we want to do it with. Sound familiar? No wonder our world is in the shape it's in. When we act as if we were God everything falls apart. Especially when we misuse the gift of our sexuality, no wonder the very fabric of our individual lives and the life of our society is unraveling.

How do we begin to knit it back together? We need to follow the commandments, especially the Sixth Commandment, again, because it is so very basic. If we begin to value the gift of our sexuality as God wishes, family life will become stronger; children will have both a father and a mother, the many diseases associated with misuse of sexuality will be dramatically reduced, and, most importantly, the true meaning and purpose of this gift will once more reflect the very life of God.

As we examine our consciences in the area of sexuality, I recommend, as a tremendous help, consulting the New Catechism of the Catholic Church. The insights we find there will give us not only great information but also encouragement in living the life to which God has called us.

SEVENTH COMMANDMENT:
THOU SHALT NOT STEAL.

The Seventh Commandment deals with how we are to treat the property of others. We are not to take what belongs to another and we are not to withhold from another what is his due. Also included in this commandment is the prohibition against cheating. There are all kinds of loopholes our society offers to get around all of these things. Cheating on our taxes is allowed because the government has more money than any of us. This same reasoning is used when we are undercharged at any store. We would be foolish according to societal dictates to call the error to the store's attention. In regard to cheating on an exam, well, that's simply to be expected. So many excuses! Such dishonesty! Stealing is stealing, just as telling a lie is a lying. Certainly there are degrees of gravity in stealing as well as in lying. However, if we are untrustworthy in small matters will we be trustworthy in big ones? Sound familiar?

I would imagine that most of us are basically honest and that for the most part we don't steal from others. However, I would be willing to bet that there is one area of dishonesty, of stealing, which the majority of people, especially Catholics, are very guilty of. This is the area of tithing, giving 10% of what we have been given by God back to Him. If we are not tithing we are literally stealing from God. It certainly is bad enough when we steal from each other, but when we steal from God Himself! Not a good thing! God has asked us from the Old Testament on to show our dependence on Him by giving a tithe of all that we have been given. In fact tithing has very little to do with the money. Tithing has *everything* to do with showing our dependence upon God and complying in obedience with what He has asked of us. (I refer you back to the first chapter of this book, "Y2G," for an extensive explanation of and rationale for tithing.) I'm certain that no one sets out to steal from God. It's more of a bad habit that we fall into. It's something that happens when we listen to the world tell us that we made all this money and so we can use it in any way we so choose. First of all the reality is the only thing that we can legitimately claim as our own is our sin. Everything else, including our money and all of our possessions has been given to us by God. To tithe is to give 10% "right off the top" as an offering to God. If we don't tithe, not only are we being disobedient to God but we're also saying to Him that we can take care of ourselves and our families without His help and blessing. When we look at the whole thing in this way can any of us afford not to tithe? Another part of this same reality is: if we steal so cavalierly from God, no wonder it doesn't really bother us when we cheat and steal from each other. If we still are making excuses for not tithing, no wonder we can rationalize, to soothe our consciences, why we cheat and steal from others. I believe it's the old white lie syndrome.

So, when we come before the Lord in preparing ourselves for Reconciliation, before we so quickly dismiss our involvement in stealing from others, maybe we need to examine if or how we have been stealing from the Other. If this is the case, our need for God's forgiveness is very real.

EIGHTH COMMANDMENT:
THOU SHALT NOT BEAR FALSE WITNESS
AGAINST THY NEIGHBOR.

This commandment has to do basically with lying. We tell a lie when we purposely say something that is not true or when we withhold the truth from someone who has a right to it. Included in the Eighth Commandment is also the preservation of a person's good name. The two major sins, which pertain here, are detraction and calumny. Detraction is telling what is true about a person to someone who has no right to the information, and, in giving this information, the reputation of this person is seriously compromised.

Calumny is simply telling a lie about someone, destroying that person's good name. Although neither of these sins literally takes the life of someone, they can and many times do kill a person's good reputation. These are very serious sins.

It seems that in our society today we sin the most against this commandment. Gossip is rampant and it is so commonplace that we think nothing of it. It has truly become a way of life for most of us. We also need to look at how we hurt others with our sarcasm. Although this is certainly an accepted form of humor, sarcasm gets a laugh at the expense of another. One of the best antidotes against gossip and sarcasm is silence. Truly, if we listen to all we say, most likely about 80% of it needed be said at all.

There are three questions, which we might ask ourselves each time we're tempted to talk about someone. How we answer them, will determine whether we open our mouths at all. The first question: Does it need to be said? Notice, I don't say do we need to say it, because we can rationalize our way into saying anything. Everyone is entitled to our opinion, whether they ask for it or not! No, we don't have to comment on everything and everyone. Most of the time silence is not only golden but it also prevents us from sinning with our mouths. The second question: Is what I'm saying giving honor and glory to God? With what I am saying am I building someone up or tearing someone down? The majority of the time we talk about others we are *not* building them up! Usually we are adding our own to criticism to that which has already been said. This is one of the easiest questions to answer. If we're speaking kindly about someone then we are giving honor and glory to God. If we're not speaking kindly, then we're not. Simple. Not easy, but simple. The third question: Would I say what I'm saying if Jesus were standing in front of me? If question one and question two don't silence us when we find ourselves gossiping, this third one will. Of course we wouldn't say anything bad or disparaging about someone if Jesus were right in front of us! The reality is that not only is Jesus always in front of us, He's behind us, He's above us, and He's *in* us by reason of our baptism. There is nowhere we go that He is not there. We can never hide from Him. All that we think and say, we think and say in His presence.

Bearing false witness against our neighbor will be a constant temptation for us living in the world as we do. We need to realize how susceptible we are to this and how easily we can slip into it. We also need to look at the "near occasion" for this sin. Perhaps there are certain people in our lives that our just being around them can lead us into the sin of detraction or calumny. If this is the case, for our own spiritual welfare, we need not to be around them so often. Will this be difficult? Yes. Is it worth it? Of course! Maybe another question we need to keep in the back of our mind is this: Is anyone worth going to hell over? Are our friends and acquaintances leading us closer to heaven or away from it? We need to bring all of this before the Lord for His forgiveness and healing and strength.

NINTH COMMANDMENT:
THOU SHALT NOT COVET THY NEIGHBOR'S WIFE.

The Ninth Commandment goes with the Sixth Commandment. This commandment, however, deals with what is within our hearts rather than with the overt act of adultery. It includes the "lusting after," the regarding of the wife (or husband) of another not only as a sex object but also the desire to break the vows of marriage, and so to commit a sacrilege—the desecration of a Sacrament. What is involved in this commandment is the whole area of concupiscence, allowing our thoughts and desires to overcome us. Just as we are forbidden by the Sixth Commandment to have sexual intercourse with another if we or that person is married, which is adultery; or if we or that person is not married, which is fornication; by the Ninth Commandment we are forbidden to harbor such thoughts and desires in our hearts, even if we do not act upon them.

Both of these commandments are given to us to preserve the beauty of the marriage relationship between spouses and to insure the stability of family life. As we know, our society scoffs at both these commandments and the reasons for which they are given to us. The whole idea of a permanent life-long commitment of love, support, and mutual affection between a husband and wife is a fantasy as far as our world is concerned. Again, the devil wants to destroy marriage and family life. So, if he cannot persuade us to actually misuse our sexuality, he will at least try to tempt us to think about it; because, if we think about it long enough, human weakness being what it is, we might move from thought and desire to the act itself. Either way, the devil gets what he wants, the degradation of our sexuality and the possible destruction of the Sacrament of Marriage.

We play right into the devil's hands when we let our guard down. We need to acknowledge that temptations to misuse our sexuality and to break our wedding vows are constantly and insidiously surrounding us daily in the press and especially in movies and on television. And after we acknowledge these temptations are ever-present we need to ask Our Lord's help to overcome them and to recommit ourselves to a pure and chaste life.

TENTH COMMANDMENT:
THOU SHALT NOT COVET THY NEIGHBOR'S GOODS.

This commandment focuses really on greed and envy and jealousy, which we hold in our hearts for the possessions of another. Just as the Seventh Commandment prohibits us from the actual taking what belongs to another, the Tenth Commandment prohibits us from harboring such a desire within us even if we do not act upon it. This commandment deals with matters of the heart and it points out an ingrained tendency to look at what others have instead of being grateful for what is ours. It truly speaks of our ingratitude and shows how easily we become possessed by our possessions. Of course our society, whose motto is "Whoever dies with the most toys wins," can't fathom the necessity to even intimate that greed and amassing as much as we can is in any way harmful to the human spirit. "Keeping up with the Joneses" is simply a fact of life, or it used to be. Now our goal has to be doing *better* than the Joneses.

Being inundated constantly with this kind of brainwashing and mind-numbing propaganda, it's no wonder that we're tempted to look at this commandment as well as the others as not applicable to our lives today. It may have applied to the lives of the people at the time the commandments were given, but it certainly doesn't apply to us now. This is truly a great temptation we face! Fighting against out-of-control materialism, either actual or desired will require much of us and demand our complete dependence upon God. When we are tempted to become discouraged in the fight and believe that we may as well go along with the crowd, we need to remember that "with God all things are possible."

The Ten Commandments, which God, out of His Fatherly love and concern, has given us, are the greatest guide we have. He gave them to us as a kind of "operations' manual" for us to live well and in peace and with joy here on earth so that we can one day be with Him again in heaven. When Jesus came He not only reiterated and upheld these Commandments but He also showed us how to live them out as His Father intended, not just following the letter of the Law as the Pharisees did. Jesus made these wonderful life-giving commandments come alive for us. By His own example of putting them into practice, He showed us that they liberate our spirit and bring joy and peace to our heart. He wanted us to realize what freedom there is in obedience to the Law of God.

Our response needs to be one of tremendous gratitude to our God for loving us so much that He would give us such gifts as the Ten Commandments. The best way to thank Him is to recommit ourselves each day to following these Laws of His Love.

GOD ONLY KNOWS

Many times, as a rather off-handed statement, we've said or heard the phrase, "God only knows." In saying this, most of the time in frustration or exasperation, we simply mean that we have no clue as to what's happened, is happening, or is going to happen. However, when we look at that statement at face value, I think we can quite literally say that it is one of the truest things we could ever say. Only God and God only knows—everything. When we say this with faith it is truly a great statement of our submission to the Will of God. It says a lot about our obedience to His plan in our lives. It also proclaims something that we need to be reminded of often, *we are not God!* All of this may seem to be rather simplistic, but, given how cavalierly our society approaches anything that has to do with submission or obedience or the very belief in God, it might be a very helpful thing to consider.

One of the most important things that we need to do until Jesus comes again to take us home to heaven with Him is to proclaim with our words and our deeds that there really *is* a God, Who loves us so much that He sent His Son, Jesus, to redeem us through His passion, death, and resurrection; that, in turn, Jesus sent the Holy Spirit to give birth to the Church He founded so that He would not leave us orphaned until He comes again in glory. Now that's a task not for the faint of heart, but that is basically what Jesus is asking of us. This is an especially important task as we begin this new millennium. As we all know many thought that the world as we know it was going to end when the calendar turned 2000 (or, for those purists, 2001.) Many stockpiled food, water, generators, batteries, and other survival necessities. Many just held their breath hoping for the best. When New Year's Day came and went for both of those years, some breathed a sigh of relief and some, I think, maybe were a little disappointed. Then came September 11, 2001. The world as we knew it did go away. We are definitely a different people. We came together as a nation like we hadn't for a long time and we began to pray again to our God for healing and consolation. Unfortunately, much of that "coming together" and that turning again to prayer has decreased the further we get from

September 11th. No matter how far we've come since that day, the evil, which happened that day is certainly a reality. We were reminded of its existence, and, as we were, we instinctively turned to the only One Who can and has defeated it, God. This turning back to God should really tell us something about ourselves—that no matter how far we wander from Him, we remember where to go when everything is falling apart and when we absolutely are at a loss for how to deal with this disintegration in our lives. We know "in our gut" where to turn because God is the One Who created us. As St. Augustine said, "We are made for Thee, Oh God, and restless will we be until we rest in Thee." Because of our human weakness we believe that we really are the masters of our own destiny, that we can handle everything that is thrown our way, that there is nothing we can't solve, that we *can* stand alone, that we really do know it all, or will know it all given enough time. That's our weakness. That's what gets us into trouble. Our strength is realizing how foolish we are to think we are in control of anything. Our strength lies is accepting the fact that we are not God.

The gift that we, who are followers of Jesus, can be to the rest of our world is priceless and essential. We know with all our hearts that Jesus *is* the answer and the solution for the disintegration of society and for the soul-numbing fear that continues to spread with every new conflict or terrorist attack. We can show everyone whom to turn to in every crisis. We can assure them that we don't have to know the solution to all of what's happening in the world. We can assure them, by the way we live, by our attitude, by our outlook on things, that God <u>does</u> exist and that He *does* know what's happening and that He is and will continue to take care of us. All of this comes down to our trusting in God's Providence and our being obedient to what He asks of us. Actually, at least for me, it seems to be a no-brainer. How our world has handled, or has tried to handle, things so far, hasn't worked. Why not finally turn to the only One Who can? Only God and God only knows! If we allow Him to be God, then everything *will* work towards the good. How? I don't know. God only knows!!! If we need reassurance about all of this, it might be helpful to read, or re-read, the Book of Job in the Old Testament. Job's world also began to crumble around him.

He, too, couldn't understand the "why" or the "how" of all that was happening to him; and, more importantly, he couldn't see how it was ever going to change for the better. Sound familiar? I encourage you to read the Book of Job.

As you can see, we have our task laid out for us. It won't be easy, anything worthwhile never is. Until He comes again, Jesus wants to use us as His sign to the world of His mercy, of His forgiveness, and of His compassion. It is our task, our simple duty, to live lives of holiness, of faithfulness, of obedience, and of trust. Until He comes again, Jesus will use us as His hands, His voice, and His heart for the world. All we have to do is say, "Yes!"

A PRAYER FOR HEALING

God, Our Loving Father, we thank You for Your gracious Mercy and for Calling us Your children. And so we, Your children, ask that You would Send Your Spirit of healing into the brokenness of our bodies, of our Minds, of our hearts, of our souls, of our spirits, of our wills, of our Intellects, and of our emotions. Heal us, dear Father, in the area of our Lives in which we most need Your healing touch. Drive far from us any Influence of the evil one and deliver us from all of his snares. Send Your Holy angels to guard and protect us, and break down within our hearts any Barriers that are keeping us far from you. We pray also, dear Father, for All of our loved ones and for all of those who have asked our prayers. Send Your Spirit of healing to them at this moment wherever they may be. Heal the brokenness of their bodies, of their minds, of their hearts, of their Souls, of their spirits, of their wills, of their intellects, and of their Emotions. Heal them, dear Father, in the area of their lives in which they Most need Your healing touch. Drive far from them any influence of the Evil one and deliver them from all of his snares. Send Your holy angels to Guard and protect them, and break down within their hearts any barriers That are keeping them far from You. We ask these blessings of healing, Dear Father, for ourselves and for them in the Name of Jesus, Your Son And our Saving Lord, according to Your Will and our need and for Your Greater honor and glory.   AMEN.